QUESTIONS

Category: Business & Economics

Description: Ask questions that make the sale. You will become an expert at not only asking well thought out questions but you will carefully listen to everything your customer says. You will learn to rehearse the questions that get the results you are aiming for, which is building a relationship and becoming an important part of your customer's business. Benjamin Franklin's 13-week self improvement program will guarantee your success

Copyright Bob Oros-2017
ISBN 978-1-105-22275-7

Written and published by Bob Oros

QUESTIONS 1

Questions Ask questions that make the sale..................................5

Biggest complaints 5

What to ask early in the sales call 7

What is a "History Question"..9

Did I catch you at a bad time?..10

Ask why 14

Seven word phrase...17

What are the two types of selling? 20

Opening new accounts...29

Turn off the cell phone 33

Questions: Ask questions that make the sale 40

My 4% improvement objective:...41

What the entire course will do for you 42

Ben Franklin's system 43

Questions

Ask questions that make the sale

Biggest complaints

What are the biggest complaints customers have about sales people?

Too pushy.

Poor follow up.

Lack of product knowledge.

Poor presentation planning.

Those are the ones that are usually brought up when asking sales people what they think. However, one of the biggest complaints is not surprising: we talk too much. One of the most difficult things for many sales people to do is listening to their customers. The reason we talk too much is understandable. We called on the customer and asked for some of their time. This sets up a professional expectation on the part of the buyer. "You asked for my time, now tell me why you want it."

The pressure then falls on the sales person to deliver a presentation. This is the point in the selling process that separates the amateur from the professional. The amateur mistakenly believes that selling and talking are the same thing. The professional knows that you cannot sell anything until you first know what the customer wants. How can this be accomplished?

Instead of starting off the meeting talking about our products, services or company, start off by asking a few questions. "I am here to talk about how some of our services might be of benefit, however, before I start do you mind if I ask a few questions?"

The most compelling selling message we can deliver is not that you have something great to sell. It is "I understand what you are trying to accomplish." Find out what they want, where they are going and who they are.

Remember these famous words: "Whoever talks the most during a sales presentation ends up with the product."

What to ask early in the sales call

One thing about our customers that we all agree on - they have long memories. Ten years ago someone from your company may have made a mistake with this customer. It could have been anything from not receiving a credit to a phone call not being returned. If you are going to talk about a new product there may have been something about the broker or supplier that previously upset the customer.

The initial questions should always try to uncover any over riding objection the prospect or customer might have. Until we clear this objection away, our presentation, no matter how good or convincing it is, will fall on deaf ears. Many times it is necessary to make more than one call on a prospect before they are ready to buy or before we qualify them as someone who would be profitable for us to work with. The initial call should always start by gaining information.

Many sales presentations are designed to go through the entire presentation before handling the objections that are sure to arise. Once again any objections your potential customer has for not giving you an order should be handled first. The reason is simple: If there is some obstacle that seems insurmountable, your prospect will not hear anything else you have to say until you deal with it.

In the back of the prospects mind, maybe not even consciously, they will be thinking that whatever you say doesn't really count, because there is an overriding reason they cannot give you the business anyway. As long as an obstacle blocks your path, you will never get past it until you bring it out in the open and deal with it. The only way you can bring this obstacle out in to the open so you can deal with it is by asking questions.

What is a "History Question"

Once we have uncovered and removed any over riding objections we move into the "history question". This is the most important and valuable question a "Cutting Edge" sales person can learn to use. The history question is used to find out what their last purchase was based on. For example if you were talking to a new account you would ask: "What were the things that made you decide on your supplier?" or "What made you decide on your menu item, your menu price, your last marketing campaign?" Once they tell you they are also telling you exactly what you need to say to sell them again.

Sometimes we have to use a "focus" question first to let the customer know that we are prepared to make a presentation. A focus question will also let the customer know that we are interested in their point of view so we can "focus" on what interests them. It is important to let them know that we are prepared to give them the information, or solve the problem, that we implied when we first made the appointment. However, it is more important to find out what is on their mind before we start talking. For example: I am here to show you how to lower your labor cost as we discussed on the phone, however, it would help me if I could get your perspective on a few things first. How much would you like to realistically lower your labor cost and how do you think it could best be accomplished?

Did I catch you at a bad time?

A customer's first objective is to take control of the sales person. This is usually accomplished by having a ready-made objection. Try this reverse psychological questioning approach.

Do you know that you can't sell anybody anything! That's right, it can't be done. No one can sell you or me anything we don't want. And if they do, we will more than likely take it back or resent the fact that they persuaded us to buy it in the first place.

No, you can't sell anybody anything, but here is what you can do. And with this concept your life is about to get a whole lot easier. All you have to do is help people make good decisions. And the good decision will be to buy from YOU.

Here's what I mean.

When you buy software how do you make your decision? You look over the package or point of sale and read the benefits the software will provide you. You read the problems it will help you solve. And most importantly, you will see a grid with product comparisons. After you study all the information the packaging provides, you make your decision.

Ask yourself this question: Why would someone want to buy products and services from me? Once you have your complete list of benefits you are ready to make your grid, like they do on the software package.

The next step is to take control by approaching your customer with a negative comment. For example, "This product may not be for you."

I know, I know, that is the exact opposite of how you have been taught to sell. But consider this. Regardless of what a sales person says, a customer or prospect has a natural tendency to disagree and gain control of the conversation. By making a negative statement you can actually get a positive response. On the other hand, if we make a positive statement they will respond with a negative statement.

Let me give you a couple of examples and let you decide.

Let's say you are going to help the armed forces recruiting efforts. Their normal approach has been to try and convince someone to join by presenting all the benefits. Here is the negative approach I am talking about:

"The Army may not be for you! Why not get the facts, see if you qualify, and then make a good sound decision as to whether this would be a good career choice."

Do you see the psychology behind this approach?

"The Army may not be for you."

What does that statement provoke? It makes you ask the question: Why not? Why wouldn't it be for me? It makes the prospect wonder what the facts are, what information do they have that will help me make a good decision. It doesn't insult my intelligence by assuming that they know what I want. It lowers the resistance that comes natural when someone is being presented with a sales pitch.

"Why not get the facts."

This implies a "no obligation" investigation into what they have that I might be interested in. It peaks my interest without undue pressure. And it takes much of the pressure off the seller as well. Instead of having the image of a high pressure sales person, the recruiter becomes a career consultant by presenting their facts and using their comparison grid to help the prospect make a good decision.

"See if you qualify."

This provokes a challenge. No one likes to be in a position of not being qualified.

Like a good lawyer, you always want to take control by asking questions that you know what your response will be. Here are a few more examples you can use to test the concept.

How would you answer these negative questions?

Did I catch you at a bad time?

I have a new, high quality product, but you may not want to look at it?

I have three consulting packages, but you may not want to look at the most expensive one?

Ask why

In buying or selling it is not always smart to be too decisive or knowledgeable. This is one of the classic strategies - it is well used by seasoned sales people.

This strategy is used to draw you out with the aim of extracting more information from you. You are up against a smooth buyer when this is used against you.

You will get better answers if you are slow to understand. The trouble is that most of us want to look good. We find it hard to say, "I don't know" or "tell me that again."

An excellent example of asking for help: While I was sitting in a sales managers office getting ready to go to lunch with him, his secretary announced that his 11:45 life insurance appointment was here. I volunteered to leave, but he said it would only take a few minutes and to stay put.

The young insurance man entered the office, handed the sales manager an application and said, "You don't want to buy any life insurance, do you?" That is considered the poorest choice of words a sales person could ever use.

The sales manager couldn't believe what he was hearing. He sat the insurance man down and for 15 minutes lectured him on how to sell. He told him how to use features and benefits, family protection, cash build up and education funds.

The sales manager said he was going to buy $250,000 additional coverage and began showing the young insurance man how to fill out the application. The sales manager handed the insurance salesman the completed application along with a deposit check and said, "Son, I hope you have learned never to use that opening question again?"

As the insurance man was leaving, his signed application and deposit check in hand, he turned to the sales manager and said, "Oh, I never use that line, unless I'm calling on a sales manager."

Customer surveys are basically useless because people only tell you what you want to hear. Here is a magic question that will reveal the true feelings of your customer: How can I make it better?

Q: How has our service been? A: It has been fine. Q: How can we make it better?

By using this additional question you are able to extract the real information you need. With this information you may be able to make changes or improvements before its too late and you lose the customer to a more creative competitor.

You will get better answers if you are slow to understand. The trouble is that most of us want to look good. We find it hard to say, "I don't know" or "tell me that again."

Seven word phrase

This seven-word strategy has the power to save you thousands of dollars each year. If you use this seven-word question seven times you will save money. I use this strategy every chance I get.

Here is an example. I had a meeting in San Jose, California and when I called to reserve a room the price was $289 for one night. My reply was $289 FOR ONE NIGHT? I live in Oklahoma, that's a month's rent, including utilities! The lowest I could get them down to was $269. Instead of taking the room I decided to drive around looking for something a little less expensive. I came across a name brand hotel and asked the clerk how much a room was for the night. The woman behind the counter said $189. I decided to use the "is that the best you can do" question - also called "the squeeze" - and see if I could get a discount. My first tactic was to use price shock. She came down to $169. Next I asked her if that was the best she could do. She came down to $149. Then I asked her if she had any specials going on and she lowered the price to $99. I asked her one more time if she could do any better explaining that I was on a tight budget and anything over $100 (including taxes) would cause me a lot of problems. She lowered the price to $89! TWO HUNDRED DOLLARS less than what the first price I was given when I first came to town!

There are several things she could have done to get a higher price.

First, she came down too easy and too fast. If she had been slightly reluctant I would have stopped asking for a lower price.

Second, she could have said it was obvious that you have not checked the price at the Hilton - I would have stopped asking for the lower price.

Third, she could have said she had to check with the manager (higher authority) and walked in the back room for a moment - returning, she could have said the manager would not let her go any lower (even if the manager was not in the office).

Fourth, when I was shocked at her price, she could have acted surprised at my shock. This would have stopped me by making me feel slightly embarrassed - well, maybe a normal person would have been embarrassed.

This seven-word statement has saved me an untold amount of money over the years. I was recently in Los Angeles working with a group of sales people and the "is that the best you can do strategy" was thoroughly explained. One of the sales people called me the next day and said he was able to save TWO THOUSAND DOLLARS on a software program he was buying. I was working with a group of sales people in Las Vegas and a sales person called me the next day and said he was able to save EIGHT HUNDRED DOLLARS on a landscape project he was purchasing for his new home. I was in Allentown Pennsylvania and one of the managers called me the next day and said he was able to save FIVE THOUSAND DOLLARS on a contract he was working on. What should you do when someone asks you if that is the best you can do? Simply say yes.

What should you do when someone asks you if that is the best you can do? Simply say yes.

What are the two types of selling?

Do you know the difference between the two distinct types of selling?

The single call close is when you have one opportunity to make the sale. For example, home remodeling. In one 3 or 4 hour period you build rapport, present your product, overcome all the objections, close and leave with the check.

The multiple call close is when you may have to call on a potential account for weeks, or even months, before you are able to build rapport and present your products.

They are two very different types of selling. If you apply the principles of the single call close in a multiply call situation, you will be perceived as "pushy." If you apply the principles of the multiply call close in a single call situation you will starve to death.

If you follow this process to the letter - you will open more new business than you can handle.

You will make more money for you and your family - you will be recognized at the sales meetings - you will win the contest - and you will get your sales manager off your case.

New business is the life of your business. There is no faster way to exceed your sales plan than to aggressively go after new accounts.

If you are having difficulty getting new business it will ALWAYS BE DUE TO ONE OR MORE OF FIVE REASONS.

Learn what they are - work with them - and you will reach your goal.

The sale MUST be made in five steps.

Jump ahead - skip a step - and you will not make the sale.

As I said, if you apply the PRINCIPLES of the single call close to a multiply call close situation you will be perceived as too aggressive and visa versa.

However, the PROCESS is the same.

Here is the PROCESS - THE FIVE STEPS YOU MUST TAKE.

1. YOU MUST SELL YOURSELF FIRST. As a buyer - if I don't like YOU - I don't care how low your price is - I don't care how well known your company is - I don't care

what products you sell. If I don't like you I will not buy from you.

How do you sell yourself?

You have to express more interest in the buyer than anyone ever has. You have to be more interested in them than their own mother. You have to research their business. Find out what their goals and objectives are. Find out what they do in their spare time. Learn the name of their kids and their dog. Find out what their hobbies are. Find out how long they have been in business - how did they get started - what challenges did they have to overcome to reach the level of success they now have.

Until the potential customer feels comfortable with you, don't make the mistake of jumping ahead to the next step. Any attempt to sell a person who is not sold on you first will end in failure and frustration.

This first step may be accomplished in 15 minutes or 15 weeks.

Let's take a lesson from our friends in the car business. If a customer enters the show room and the sales person has not built rapport WITHIN FIFTEEN MINUTES the sales person will pass the customer over to someone else. They know a car will never be sold unless they make it past the first step.

Here are two perfect example of something that happened to me this week - one at a restaurant - one at a store.

My wife and I stopped to have breakfast a few days before Thanksgiving at a Cracker Barrel restaurant. The waitress asked us if we were having company over for Thanksgiving dinner. We said we were having a only few people over. She then suggested that we bring them to the Cracker Barrel for Thanksgiving and save all the work.

She did a perfect job of selling herself first by being interested in whether we were having company rather than simply trying to jump into her pitch about their holiday dinner. It only took her about 15 seconds.

Here is the second example.

I really enjoy a fireplace - but I hate to clean it up and take care of the wood. I stopped at a gas company to ask about a gas burning log they were advertising. As the sales person approached he asked if I had been to Alaska. I didn't realize I was wearing a shirt I had bought while working with the Alaska division of Food Services of America. I said yes and for fifteen minutes he asked me questions about my trip.

I was thinking to myself that I really like this guy - he is actually interested in my trip. He sold himself long before we ever started to discuss the benefits of a gas fireplace.

Remember, no one will pay you a penny to listen to your sales pitch. However, consultants are paid thousands of dollars to ask questions.

Don't go into a potential new account and try to sell your company or products until you sell yourself.

2. SELL YOUR COMPANY. Don't bypass this second step by assuming the prospect knows all about your

company. For the prospect to even consider buying from you he or she has to weigh your company against your competitor. They have to make a comparison. They have to know the things that make you different. They need solid facts, not fiction.

Instead of asking, "Are you familiar with our company?" ask, "Do you know much about our company?" Even if your prospects are familiar with your company, they usually don't know much about it. Now you have the opportunity to tell them.

You must be like a lawyer presenting your case to the jury. Don't build your presentation on weak points.

Here you can take a lesson from the folks who sell software. Look on any software box and you will see a "grid." You will see a list of features along the left column. On the top you will see the names of their competitors. By going over this comparison list the potential customer will be presented FACTS AND PROOF that will help them make the decision you want hear.

Never use statements like "we are the biggest" or "we are the best." As soon as you blurt out one of these over used phrases you have immediately unsold yourself. They are thinking, "says who?"

Make a list of at least 20 things you and your company will do for this person once a mutually beneficial program is put together.

3. SELL YOUR PRODUCTS. Never fall into the trap of giving a price on something when you are in steps one and two. Your prospect will probably ask for a price on a specific item. Don't give it to them. Tell them you don't know the price. Tell them you must first learn about their business. You must look at the overall picture. Present your products as solutions to their problems. Always have examples and success stories of other customers who are successfully using your product line.

4. PRESENT YOUR PRICING. After you have asked a dozen questions and the time has come to suggest products, don't fall into the price trap. If you are more

expensive be prepared to JUSTIFY RATHER THAN IMMEDIATELY DISCOUNT.

If your prices are slightly higher than your competitor FIND OUT WHY. What are they leaving out or putting in that is changing the value.

This is the point where you need to know how to negotiate. All buyers want to feel good about making a purchase or changing vendors. You must know how to make them feel good about their decision to change.

5. THE TIMING IS NOT RIGHT. If you have done a good job of going through the first four steps and the prospect says the timing is not right - then the timing is not right. Find out what their time frame is. Ask for a specific date and time for you to call them back. Don't leave without a follow up plan. If you have NOT done a good job of going through the first four steps THE TIMING WILL NEVER BE RIGHT.

Opening new accounts

"I forgot they were coming!"

"I wonder how long this is going to take."

"My production supervisor is on vacation."

"My office manager called in sick this morning!"

"YIKES! Look at all the stuff they have with them!"

"There are two of them - they will probably never stop talking."

"This is going to take forever - I've got to do something - fast."

"I see they have a price book - good - I know how to get rid of them."

"I'll get a price quote on something and tell them they are way too high.""

If you are having the door slammed in your face before you even have a chance to say hello - you may be doing it wrong.

Let me explain.

Why do you go to the office before an appointment and gather a ton of brochures, fill your brief case with samples, get a complete product list, take your laptop, and ask someone else to go on the sales call with you?

Your first mistake is thinking that the potential customer is remotely interested in you or what you are selling. You mistakenly think that they want to read your brochures (they don't), listen to your sales pitch (they have a hundred other things that are more pressing) and ask questions about you and your company (they really don't care). You mistakenly think that you are showing the importance you put on the appointment because there are two of you.

When they agreed to the appointment - you caught them at a weak moment. I am sure you have heard of "buyer's remorse". Let me introduce you to a new concept – "agreeing to an appointment remorse." As soon as they hang up the phone it starts - "Why did I agree to see that sales person?"

Agreeing to an appointment is like buying on a credit card - easy to make the purchase - hard to pay off. Something you said may have sparked a small interest during your initial phone conversation - that spark has long since gone out by the time you show up.

So the question is: Why do you bring all this stuff with you and why do you invite someone to go along? You might be thinking that the reason is to be prepared.

The answer is - you lack confidence. I know – that's tough to swallow – but it is the truth. Having all this stuff and bringing someone with you assures you that you will have something to talk about.

Here is a little known secret about selling. Your job is not to talk, but to listen - not to present, but to ask questions.

The first thing you have to do is lower the prospects defenses. You do this by going alone and not taking anything, or anybody, with you. No computer, no brochures, no prices, not even a brief case. This takes courage because most sales people are taught that their job is to "show and tell." When you walk into an account "unarmed" and simply ask permission to ask a few questions, there is very little pressure on the buyer and even less on you.

As a professional, you have to evaluate the account to see if it will be profitable for you to invest your time with them. You have to position yourself to be on the offensive rather than the defensive when making a new account call. If you don't have your price book and someone wants to put you on the defensive by asking for a price – simply say "I don't know" and continue to ask questions about their business.

The process of calling on an account without a lot of baggage is similar to a visit to the dentist or doctor - you would want a complete examination before getting an operation or having a tooth pulled.

The first time you try it you will feel "unprepared." That is a good sign - it means you are trying something new and at the brink of learning a new skill.

I would like to challenge you to make a few cold calls this week completely unarmed - not unprepared - just unarmed.

What are you going to talk about? You are not going to talk - you are going to ask questions.

What person in their right mind would say 'no' to a question like this: I am here to talk about YOU - do YOU mind if I ask YOU a few questions about YOUR business to see if I might be able to be of service to YOU and help YOU achieve YOUR goals?

Turn off the cell phone

Can you imagine being in the closing moments of a large, important purchase you are making with a sales person and a sales manager and just as you have one final question before you sign the deal, the sales manager takes a call on his cell?

That would tick me off enough to say "take this sale and stick it!" Well, that is exactly what happened to YOU! And that is exactly what you DID!

I recently asked people on my email list to send comments about their last car purchase. What they liked or didn't like about the sales person that sold them the car.

As I was editing and placing the comments my readers were so kind to send me there was one HUGE complaint that showed up over and over again. The biggest deal maker or deal breaker was how well the sales person listened, or did NOT listen. Without a single doubt, the most important skill a sales person can have is to listen better.

Here are just a few of the comments YOU made about this important part of the sales process:

"Great listener"

"Because the salesman listened"

"Listening to us was the key"

"Listened and keep gathering information"

"It was his listening skills that earned the sale"

"He was listening to me and my wife"

"Not listening cost him the sale"

"Asked really good questions and listened"

"He listened to what I said"

"He listened and there was no high pressure"

"TURN OFF THE CELL PHONE!!"

"He wasn't pushy and listened"

"He listened to my wife, he asked questions"

"He listened what I was looking for"

"Politely listened to my wife"

"Asking what is important to me"

"Not listening to what was wrong"

"By listening to us he made the sale"

"He was willing to listen, really listen"

"Took the time to listen to us"

"Not listening and pre-judging needs cost him the sale"

"One thing he failed to do and that was listen"

"If they only would have listened he would have sold me"

"Asked the right questions and listened carefully"

"He reinforced the fact that he was listening to me"

"He asked questions then he shut up and LISTENED"

"Had he listened to us he would have made the sale"

"He listens, he consults, he works to get me what I want"

"My salesperson listened to what I had to say"

"He listened and offered suggestions"

"He did NOT waste my time but LISTENED"

And by listen, I mean focusing on what they are saying rather than waiting for an opening to jump in and start "selling" again!

Are you guilty of talking too much and not being a great listener? If you are guilty, I guarantee, people will cross the street so they won't have to listen to your endless, meaningless, boring stories.

There is a time to talk. And that time is when you are invited to talk or you are asked a question.

Even when you give your "elevator speech" you should ask permission before you dump it in their lap. For example "My job is to help you save money in four areas of your company, would you like to know briefly what they are?" By having enough respect to ASK you will have their attention because you framed it as a QUESTION!

Here is a fact about talking and listening. The person doing the talking is actually more alert and awake because their lungs are getting more oxygen, their blood is circulating better, their mind is sharper, they are more interested in what's going on and there is even a chemical produced in the person's mind that stimulates a person as if they have taken a drug!

Don't believe me? Try this test. Get your spouse talking by bringing up something important and interesting to THEM. Really pay close ATTENTION. Ask them questions that keep them ENGAGED. Be SINCERELY interested. Lean in closer so you won't miss a word of what they are saying. Forget about yourself and what you have to say. Just be completely in the present moment without any background noise going on in your mind.

Then go out and try it with a customer. You will thank me on payday!

So let me ask you a question. Would you rather have the customer talk themselves INTO the sale by asking questions and listening, or would you rather do all the talking and talk yourself OUT of the sale?

According to YOUR comments, if you don't listen, you lose. And for goodness sakes, turn your cell phone off when you are with a customer!! What could be more important than the person RIGHT IN FRONT OF YOU!

Questions: Ask questions that make the sale

I am an expert at asking well thought out questions and I carefully listen to everything my customer says. I have rehearsed the questions that will get the results I am aiming for, which is building a relationship and becoming an important part of my customer's business. I let my customer do most of the talking and they look forward to my visit because I am so interested in them and their business. I keep careful records of the answers and information I get and review them each time I make a repeat call. The customer can almost feel my sincere interest in them.

My 4% improvement objective:

_____

_____

_____

_____

_____

_____

What the entire course will do for you

Buying all 13 books is like buying a library of 13 powerful coaching sessions that will increase every skill necessary for generating business. Once you experience the seemingly effortless improvement you will understand why there is a picture of Ben Franklin on every 100 dollar bill.

You will learn how to improve relationships, improve management skills, be more productive, generate more customers, negotiate better contracts, open new accounts, earn more profits and create more sales! Results most people only dream about! If you are a sales professional or an entrepreneur this is the perfect program to boost your sales and increase your profits.

Ben Franklin's system

In our fast paced business and personal life today it has become increasingly difficult to set aside time for self development and improving your skills. With every spare minute taken up by reading blogs, logging on to Facebook, following people on Twitter, responding to text messages and emails and constantly talking on your cell phone, there seems to be little, if any, time left for learning new skills. Even the quiet time behind the wheel of your car is no longer available with satellite radio and cell phone coverage in every corner of the country.

Even though this seems like a new problem, distractions have been around forever. Two hundred years ago a man by the name of Ben Franklin had the same problem. He concluded that it was not a matter of distractions as much as a matter of focus. He set out to solve the problem and created the most effective system for self improvement ever invented.

Ben Franklin gives credit for all his success and accomplishments to the implementation of this system for the success he sought after. Despite being born into a poor family and only receiving two years of formal schooling, Ben Franklin became a successful printer, scientist, musician, author and one of the founding fathers of the United States. Ben Franklin is considered to have been one of the most persuasive and successful people in the history of the United States. He was a very skilled sales person, marketer, negotiator and copywriter. Skills that every business owner, professional person, manager and marketer should have.

In the year 1723, Ben Franklin, at the age of seventeen, arrived in Philadelphia without a penny to his name. At age 42, he retired, wealthy, the first self made millionaire in the country. Few people, before or since have ever been as successful as Benjamin Franklin. He gave credit for his many inventions and business successes to his system for self improvement he created when he was 20 years old.

The key to Franklin's success was his drive to constantly improve himself and accomplish his ambitions. In order to accomplish his goal, Franklin developed and committed himself to a personal improvement program that consisted of mastering 13 principles.

When he was seventy-nine years old, Benjamin Franklin wrote more about this idea than anything else that ever happened to him in his entire life. He felt that he owed all his success and happiness to this one thing. Franklin wrote: "I hope, therefore, that some of my descendants may follow the example and reap the benefit."

Since success is developed by performing small and seemingly insignificant acts, you can use this method by reading and putting into practice the 13 skills that will guarantee your success in sales with scientific certainty.

This program takes advantage of Franklin's system and applies it to improving your skills as a sales professional. This program will show you how to dominate your market by first dominating yourself. By focusing on the 13 skills that make up a highly effective and successful sales professional. As these skills are improved your results and sales increases will also show a dramatic improvement.

The goal of going through the program the first time is to increase each skill by only four percent. With the accomplishment of this small improvement in each skill or attitude your overall improvement will be 52%. Those are results most people only dream about. However, you can accomplish this by investing as little as 45 minutes once a week reading one book and then focusing on improving the single skill during the rest of the week. The second week by reading the second book and focusing on that single skill during the week and so on until all 13 weeks are completed.

You can write the single word on the back of your business card and tape it to your dash board as a reminder. You can put this one word on your smart phone as a reminder as well as on your email signature, your Facebook page or you can even have something worthwhile to tweet about. One word, one week, one skill, one "I am" statement, 4% improvement objective and your subconscious mind will receive the message through all the clutter and act on it.

After the first time through the process you can do as Ben Franklin suggests and go through the program a second, third and fourth time. Get your whole sales team on the same page at the same time and you will experience a whirlwind of new excitement and new business. Or get a like minded colleague and join forces with accountability and focus.

Achieve a 52% improvement

Using Franklin's scientific program for learning your objective is to improve 4% in each area over 13 weeks.

1. Attitude Define what you want and go after it.
2. Respect Earn respect-no more comfort zone.
3. Service Help customers build their business.
4. Urgency Be enthusiastic get things done now.
5. Confidence Remove restrictions and limitations.
6. Persistence Keep going and never give up.
7. Planning Get big results by setting big goals.
8. Questions Ask questions that make the sale.
9. Attention Get attention with irresistible offers.
10. Presenting Give reasons why they should buy.
11. Objections Remove every roadblock to the sale.
12. Closing Ask for the order and get paid.
13. Follow up Remove all hope for competitors.

About the author Bob Oros (BobOros.com),

Bob Oros has been a full time speaker and author since 1992 with over 2,000 speaking engagements in all 50 states and several international locations as well as the author of 21 books on sales. Prior to starting his speaking career, Bob served six years in the US Navy as a Communications Specialist and then worked his way from a street sales person to the position of National Sales Manager for a Fortune 200 company.

CSP Award: Bob was awarded the designation of Certified Speaking Professional (CSP) by the National Speakers Association and the International Federation for Professional Speakers. Fewer than 10% of all speakers worldwide qualify for this award.

PWA Member: Bob is a member of the Professional Writers Alliance.

www.ingramcontent.com/pod-product-compliance
Lightning Source LLC
Chambersburg PA
CBHW072256170526
45158CB00003BA/1088